JOURNEY FROM SALVATION TO WORSHIP

Workbook

JOURNEY FROM SALVATION TO WORSHIP

Workbook

DELSHANNA MOORE

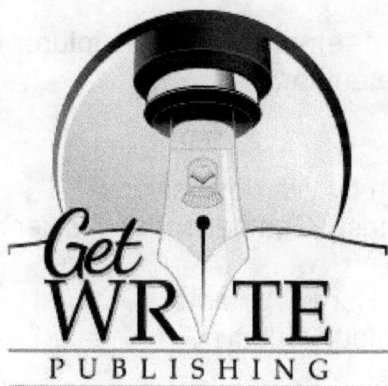

Get
WR TE
PUBLISHING

Journey from Salvation to Worship Workbook

Copyright © 2017, 2018 by DelShanna Moore
Published by GET WRITE Publishing, Dallas, TX

Printed in the United States of America.
ISBN 978-0-9994648-6-1

Unless otherwise noted, all Scripture quotations are taken from the King James Version of the Bible © 1988 by Liberty University.

The italicized emphasis in Scripture quotations is added by the author.

Cover Design by Warrior Designs
Edited by Christy Cumberlander-Walker and Dr. Kathy Howard
Hair: I'jah K. Harris-Williams
Stylist: Antoinette Griffin

TABLE OF CONTENTS

If you confess with your mouth
that Jesus is Lord
and believe in your heart that God
raised him from the dead,
you will be saved.
Romans 10:9, NLT

When I was a child,
I spake as a child,
I understood as a child,
I thought as a child:
but when I became a man,
I put away childish things.
1 Corinthians 13:10

Introduction

The Journey from Salvation to Worship is personal and requires your undivided attention. Each step in your journey bears its host of celebration and reward. The day you were born was the evidence that God wanted your life to speak to the nations. The day you accepted Christ as your Savior was the day you confirmed whose banner you wave and which kingdom you were aligned with. The day you spoke in your holy language was the day you received the fire power to break curses and defeat your spiritual enemies. The day you decided to allow the Holy Spirit to guide your very life was the day you began walking with God. Each of the steps you take on your journey leads you through the phases of Journey from Salvation to Worship.

Once you have accepted Christ as your Savior, getting to know God as Creator, Jesus Christ as Savior, and Holy Spirit as Comforter becomes your life's work. However, you worship, aloud or quiet, in public or private, the critical condition of worship is that you spend enough time to establish a secure intimate relationship with God. Much like you develop intimacy with friends and family over the years of sharing life's stories, genuinely caring about each other and being in each other's presence, your worship with God requires the same diligence.

This 12-phase devotional workbook facilitates your journey from initial salvation to true worship. It is designed to help you think on the things of God and consider in depth conversations with Holy Spirit for greater insight and understanding. Each phase concludes with questions and tasks for you to complete. From listing issues to identifying your favorite scripture to making commitments to be more like Christ, this workbook is designed to capture your journey and facilitate essential change, moving you to a broader intimacy with Christ, which is worship.

How to Use This Workbook

This workbook is designed for individual, partner or small group learning and growth. As such, the questions after each phase were developed to encourage you to apply God's word to your life. Examples are provided in the written portion of each phase. These exerts compliment those provided in greater detail in the book, <u>Journey from Salvation to Worship</u>. As such, additional scriptures are provided to expand your study and understanding of God's will, way, and Word.

     Each phase has seven applications for you to respond to including making an immediate commitment towards improving your life as a Believer. Some applications require additional study or research, while others require your honest thoughts and communication about such subjects in your life. Remember, the goal is worship. Processing the reality of who we are and who we desire to be is part of our journey to worship. We cannot reach our God-ordained goals without facing our fears, speaking the truth and vowing for a better self. I recommend you complete a phase in its entirety before moving on to the next to ensure you gain the lessons and align with the growth each supports. You may choose to begin in Phase 5 rather than Phase 1 which matters least as long as you finish one phase before reading the next.

Partner Use

Having a partner allows you to both work through the phases and supports connection and accountability. When addressing change, it is easy to fall for the deceptive tricks of our mind and describe ourselves better than we are. Having a partner assists in keeping us accountable, as well as holding our partner accountable, for completing assignments and honest reflection. Finding a partner could be as easy as asking a friend or member of your church.

Small Group Use

Using this workbook in a small group creates a greater discussion and proof that you are not alone. You'll be able to share your perspectives as well as listen and learn from others. It supports the "Unity of the Spirit" and God's perfected will to bring Believers on one accord. The group should meet regularly with a plan to start and finish the Workbook together. Gathering at a location or online using meeting tools online will allow participants to gather from all part of the country and world in the <u>Journey from Salvation to Worship</u>. Because this workbook facilitates spiritual growth, it is recommended that you adhere to the following guidelines:

1. Read the Book, <u>Journey from Salvation to Worship</u>.
2. You'll need your Bible, the book, and this Workbook with your special writing pen (or pencil). You may also need a concordance or online bible study program for in-depth understanding of the scriptures.
3. Be sure to secure a quiet space to read, study and reflect. Remember, you are on a journey to defeat the enemy and he will try to fight you with distractions. *Dare to focus.*
4. Answer the questions at the end of each phase with honesty and transparency. You may share your answers at your level of comfort. Remember, you are all on the same journey to

worship, without judgment, self-righteousness or deception. Trusting people in your group is imperative and believing that God has you with others on the Journey from Salvation to Worship is the principle.

Writing your answers in the workbook or the Journey Journal is purposeful to your spiritual growth. It allows you to reflect on your progress and development in Christ. It is expected that you revisit the application of the phases as you gain greater understanding and knowledge of Christ Jesus. While you take this journey, and work to apply these scriptures to your daily walk as a Believer, the completion of this workbook does not conclude your worship experience. The Journey from Salvation to Worship is ever developing and growing in God, from glory to glory. Continuing to strengthen your relationship with God creates a deeper intimacy with Him. After months or years pass, redoing this workbook will once again, enhance your worship, as you have increased your affection with Abba Father. Let today be the first day of a life filled with worshipping...*Abba Father* (Romans 8:15) *...in spirit and truth* (John 4:24) and ...*in the beauty of holiness* (Psalm 29:2).

Your journey continues...

My Journey Dates

Date of birth: _____

Date of salvation: _____

Date of water baptism: _____

Date of Holy Ghost baptism (tongues):
_____

Date my life completely changed (my walk with God):
_____

What I like most about being a Believer is:
_____
_____
_____

What I want to share with others about being a
Believer is:
_____
_____
_____

List of favorite scriptures:
_____
_____
_____
_____

My calling/ God-given gifts:
_____
_____
_____

Phase 1

God is My Refuge

¹He that dwelleth in the secret place of the most High shall abide under the shadow of the Almighty. ² I will say of the LORD, He is my refuge and my fortress: my God; in him will I trust. ³ Surely he shall deliver thee from the snare of the fowler, and from the noisome pestilence. ⁴ He shall cover thee with his feathers, and under his wings shalt thou trust: his truth shall be thy shield and buckler. ⁵ Thou shalt not be afraid for the terror by night; nor for the arrow that flieth by day; ⁶ Nor for the pestilence that walketh in darkness; nor for the destruction that wasteth at noonday. ⁷ A thousand shall fall at thy side, and ten thousand at thy right hand; but it shall not come nigh thee. ⁸ Only with thine eyes shalt thou behold and see the reward of the wicked. ⁹ Because thou hast made the LORD, which is my refuge, even the most High, thy habitation; ¹⁰ There shall no evil befall thee, neither shall any plague come nigh thy dwelling. ¹¹ For he shall give his angels charge over thee, to keep thee in all thy ways. ¹² They shall bear thee up in their hands, lest thou dash thy foot against a stone. ¹³ Thou shalt tread upon the lion and adder: the young lion and the dragon shalt thou trample under feet. ¹⁴ Because he hath set his love upon me, therefore will I deliver him: I will set him on high, because he hath known my name. ¹⁵ He shall call upon me, and I will answer him: I will be with him in trouble; I will deliver him, and honour him. ¹⁶ With long life will I satisfy him, and shew him my salvation (Psalm 91:1-16).

God is our refuge and strength, a very present help in trouble (Psalm 46:1). What can be more reassuring than hearing God is our refuge? A refuge is a place you seek for safety and protection and for you, God is that place. That means before any harm can get to you, it has to go through God. He has developed a secret place for you to rest and find security in Him. He ensures that not only are you protected, but you are also in His presence. Of course, you know that it is practically impossible for any enemy, dagger, sword or bullet to penetrate the protective shield of God, right?

As a child of God, it is essential you recognize that you have security in Christ. The Word of God says, ***For in him we live, and move, and have our being; as certain also of your own poets have said, For we are also his offspring*** (Acts 17:28). This scripture describes you. Therefore, you must have the mentality of the protected. Otherwise, you will act and talk as though you are not safe. *If you make the LORD your refuge, if you make the Most High your shelter, no evil will conquer you; no plague will come near your home. For he will order his angels to protect you wherever you go. They will hold you up with their hands so you won't even hurt your foot on a stone* (Psalm 91:9-12, NLT).

Someone might ask, why do some Christians suffer harm? The answer is in God's Word. *He that diggeth a pit shall fall into it; and whoso breaketh an hedge, a serpent shall bite him* (Ecclesiastes 10:8). In essence, do not break the hedge of protection nor dig a pit for your brother/sister; remain under the wings of Father's protection. Just like an animal that strays from the herd becomes vulnerable to attack; a Christian that deviates from God immediately becomes easy prey to the predator, your enemy.

God boasted about Job's uprightness and perfection to the devil. *Then the LORD asked Satan, "Have you noticed my servant Job? He is the finest man in all the earth. He is blameless--a man of complete integrity. He fears God and stays away from evil* (Job 1:8, NLT). And while in transition, Job was living in fear and talking negatively. He offered sacrifices based on fear rather than in faith. *For the thing which I greatly feared is come upon me, and that which I was afraid of is come unto me. I was not in safety, neither had I rest, neither was I quiet; yet trouble came* (Job 3: 25-26). Can you see that? Job broke the hedge with language that was not consistent with God's provision for him.

Your language can affect your faith. In other words, your talk can put you in a position of an unbeliever. Job experienced this when reacting to his devastating situation. While his repugnant speech wasn't the cause of his trial, it approached becoming a problem for him. He feared the devastation and cursed the day he was born. *At last Job spoke, and he cursed the day of his birth* (Job 3:1, NLT).

When we come against trials, it is imperative that we use the Word of the Lord to express what we want. Reciting scripture such as I am **the head and not the tail**, **above and not beneath** (Deuteronomy 28:13); **all things will work out for my good** (Romans 8:28); or **he will not withhold any good thing from me** (Psalm 84:11) are helpful words to keep us in faith, believing that God is handling our situation, and we are protected.

3

For you to remain in safety, your trust must be in God and not man. Psalm 118: 8 says, *It is better to take refuge in the LORD than to trust in people* (NLT). People and their security devices can only do little in the physical realm. Any man whose esteem is in another man for safety and security is spiritually bankrupt and vulnerable, even if the trust you have is in yourself. People can be attacked and destroyed by the forces of darkness. *The LORD says: "Cursed are those who put their trust in mere humans, who rely on human strength and turn their hearts away from the LORD* (Jeremiah 17: 5, NLT).

Prayer

Heavenly Father, I thank You for Your Word that has come to me today. I am reassured that my safety and security are in You. You are my refuge and fortress, You are the one who delivers me; the one who answers me; and the one who satisfies me. Lord, I thank You for your protection for every member of my family and all those who put their trust in You, in Jesus' Name I pray. Amen.

Day 1

Write about a time when God protected you from someone or something.

_____

_____

_____

_____

_____

_____

_____

_____

_____

_____

Day 2

What attitudes hinder you from embracing God's complete protection?

_____

_____

_____

_____

_____

_____

_____

_____

_____

_____

Day 3

What can you do better to acknowledge God's protection of your life?

_____

_____

_____

_____

_____

_____

_____

_____

_____

_____

Day 4

List times in your life when you felt unprotected and thought you had no protection.

_____

_____

_____

_____

_____

_____

_____

_____

_____

_____

_____

Day 5

**Read Psalm 91. How does this influence your
fears about situations when you've felt unsafe or
unprotected?**

_____

_____

_____

_____

_____

_____

_____

_____

_____

_____

Day 6

How can you use this lesson to remind yourself that God is protecting you?

_____

_____

_____

_____

_____

_____

_____

_____

_____

_____

_____

Day 7

Since beginning this Phase, how has your perspective on life differed?

_____

_____

_____

_____

_____

_____

_____

_____

_____

_____

Phase 2

The Wisdom of God

₁The proverbs of Solomon the son of David, king of Israel; ₂To know wisdom and instruction; to perceive the words of understanding; ₃To receive the instruction of wisdom, justice, and judgment, and equity; ₄To give subtilty to the simple, to the young man knowledge and discretion. ₅A wise man will hear, and will increase learning; and a man of understanding shall attain unto wise counsels: ₆To understand a proverb, and the interpretation; the words of the wise, and their dark sayings. ₇The fear of the LORD is the beginning of knowledge: but fools despise wisdom and instruction.

The Enticement of Sin
₈My son, hear the instruction of thy father, and forsake not the law of thy mother: ₉For they shall be an ornament of grace unto thy head, and chains about thy neck. ₁₀My son, if sinners entice thee, consent thou not. ₁₁If they say, Come with us, let us lay wait for blood, let us lurk privily for the innocent without cause: ₁₂Let us swallow them up alive as the grave; and whole, as those that go down into the pit: ₁₃We shall find all precious substance, we shall fill our houses with spoil: ₁₄Cast in thy lot among us; let us all have one purse: ₁₅My son, walk not thou in the way with them; refrain thy foot from their path: ₁₆For their feet run to evil, and make haste to shed blood. ₁₇Surely in vain the net is spread in the sight of any bird. ₁₈And they lay wait for their own blood; they lurk privily for their own lives. ₁₉So are the ways of every one that is greedy of gain; which taketh away the life of the owners thereof.

Wisdom Calls Aloud

20Wisdom crieth without; she uttereth her voice in the streets: 21She crieth in the chief place of concourse, in the openings of the gates: in the city she uttereth her words, saying, 22How long, ye simple ones, will ye love simplicity? and the scorners delight in their scorning, and fools hate knowledge? 23Turn you at my reproof: behold, I will pour out my spirit unto you, I will make known my words unto you.24Because I have called, and ye refused; I have stretched out my hand, and no man regarded; 25But ye have set at nought all my counsel, and would none of my reproof: 26I also will laugh at your calamity; I will mock when your fear cometh; 27When your fear cometh as desolation, and your destruction cometh as a whirlwind; when distress and anguish cometh upon you. 28Then shall they call upon me, but I will not answer; they shall seek me early, but they shall not find me: 29For that they hated knowledge, and did not choose the fear of the LORD: 30They would none of my counsel: they despised all my reproof. 31Therefore shall they eat of the fruit of their own way, and be filled with their own devices. 32For the turning away of the simple shall slay them, and the prosperity of fools shall destroy them. 33But whoso hearkeneth unto me shall dwell safely, and shall be quiet from fear of evil (Proverbs 10:1-33).

But of him are ye in Christ Jesus, who of God is made unto us wisdom, and righteousness, and sanctification, and redemption: 1Corinthians 1:30. For some people, wisdom is a mystery. As far as they are concerned, only very few gifted individuals can be said to possess wisdom. However, this is not so. Anyone who lacks understanding can ask God, and He will grant wisdom to him or her. The Holy Spirit said through the Apostle James, *If any of you lack wisdom, let him ask of God, that giveth to all men liberally, and upbraideth not; and it shall be given him* (James 1:5). Interestingly, God has made 'His Wisdom' available to all. The heading scripture says Christ has been *...made to us wisdom, and righteousness, and sanctification, and redemption*. That means, if you want wisdom, accept Jesus Christ as Lord of your life, and you will awaken to the wisdom of God.

In your dealings in the affairs of life, you must operate with the wisdom of God. It will distinguish you from others. The Word of God says, *For the wisdom of this world is foolishness with God. For it is written, He taketh the wise in their own craftiness* (1Corinthians 3:19). The world has their ways which differ. While the ways of the world will lead to death, God's way brings peace. *There is a way which seemeth right unto a man, but the end thereof are the ways of death* (Proverbs 14:12).

Wisdom is the principal thing; therefore get wisdom: and with all thy getting get understanding (Proverbs 4:7). The wisdom of God is in His Word. As you study the scriptures daily, understanding God's Word will grant you His wisdom. Then you will be able to deal wisely with the affairs of life.

I was named a wise person. Not because of my education or socioeconomic status, but because of my intense desire to seek out the things of God with mysteries revealed. Reading the Book of Proverbs made me reconsider conversations I once entertained especially since the ways of foolishness lead to death. I also kept busy and stayed diligent in my career so not to present as slothful or lazy. Having a mindset to save for a rainy day was developed by learning from ants and other creatures who sustained without a leader.

You must have a good grasp of the characteristics of wisdom. Again, the Spirit of God through the Apostle James declares that ...***the wisdom that comes from heaven is first of all pure; then peace-loving, considerate, submissive, full of mercy and good fruit, impartial and sincere*** (James 3:17 NIV). These characteristics are the parameters with which you can measure your wisdom; if it is of God or this world.

Prayer

Most Holy Father, I thank You for granting me Your wisdom in Christ Jesus. I recognize that Your Word is Your wisdom. I declare that by the power of the Holy Spirit, I will daily study Your Word so that I will keep increasing in Your wisdom. Thus, I will deal wisely with the affairs of this life and walk upright in all that I do to Your praise and glory. I declare and decree I am filled with Your holy wisdom, in Jesus' Name I pray. Amen.

Day 1

The book of Proverbs is full of wisdom. Write out two (2) scriptures from Proverbs that you will read, study and recite daily.

_____

_____

_____

_____

_____

_____

_____

_____

_____

_____

Day 2

What foolish behavior prevents you from being open to receive from God?
Hint: There are many answers in the Book of Proverbs.

_____

_____

_____

_____

_____

_____

_____

_____

_____

_____

_____

Day 3

How can you apply wisdom in your daily walk?

_____

_____

_____

_____

_____

_____

_____

_____

_____

_____

Day 4

Give an example in the past week where you recognized God's wisdom in a situation.

_____

_____

_____

_____

_____

_____

_____

_____

_____

_____

_____

Day 5

Select 5 scriptures in Proverbs that speak to issues in your life.

_____

_____

_____

_____

_____

_____

_____

_____

_____

_____

_____

Day 6

How has applying wisdom changed situations or people in your life?

_____

_____

_____

_____

_____

_____

_____

_____

_____

_____

Day 7

Write about an era in your life where you gained wisdom.

_____

_____

_____

_____

_____

_____

_____

_____

_____

_____

Phase 3

GOD'S ARMOR

[10] *Finally, my brethren, be strong in the Lord, and in the power of his might.* [11] *Put on the whole armour of God, that ye may be able to stand against the wiles of the devil.* [12] *For we wrestle not against flesh and blood, but against principalities, against powers, against the rulers of the darkness of this world, against spiritual wickedness in high places.* [13] *Wherefore take unto you the whole armour of God, that ye may be able to withstand in the evil day, and having done all, to stand.* [14] *Stand therefore, having your loins girt about with truth, and having on the breastplate of righteousness;* [15] *And your feet shod with the preparation of the gospel of peace;* [16] *Above all, taking the shield of faith, wherewith ye shall be able to quench all the fiery darts of the wicked.* [17] *And take the helmet of salvation, and the sword of the Spirit, which is the word of God:* [18] *Praying always with all prayer and supplication in the Spirit, and watching thereunto with all perseverance and supplication for all saints;* [19] *And for me, that utterance may be given unto me, that I may open my mouth boldly, to make known the mystery of the gospel,* [20] *For which I am an ambassador in bonds: that therein I may speak boldly, as I ought to speak Ephesians 6:10-20.*

For we wrestle not against flesh and blood, but against principalities, against powers, against the rulers of the darkness of this world, against spiritual wickedness in high places *Ephesians 6:12.*

Spiritual warfare reflects battles that Christians have to fight against forces that are unseen. The devil and other cohorts of hell orchestrate attacks against humans, especially Christians. The attacks could come in the form of sickness, afflictions, fear, depression, doubts and so on. The aim of the devil in perpetuating these acts of wickedness is to steal your joy; destroy your relationships with God and to kill you.

Many believers do not believe in the supernatural, positive or negative. They do not think that earthly things can be influenced by the spiritual realm and vice versa. However, the fact remains that the spiritual world does exist, positive and negative and can impact chiefly on the affairs in the physical realm.

In the Bible, Ephesians 6:12 shows us a clear picture of the spiritual forces engaged in spiritual warfare. These bands of evil include principalities, powers, rulers of darkness, and spiritual wickedness in high places.

As a Christian, it is important you know that you are not helpless; you are not at the mercy of the devil or evil forces. God has given you powerful weapons to fight the devil from the position point of a victor. And because warfare is spiritual, we are to guard ourselves with armor and weapons that are effective for the battle. *For the weapons of our warfare are not carnal* (2 Corinthians 10:4a).

Furthermore, the Spirit through the Apostle Paul tells us how to be on the offensive. *Put on the whole armour of God, that ye may be able to stand against the wiles of the devil* (Ephesians 6:11). Continuing, He gives us the strategies to adopt so that we will be victorious always. *Wherefore take unto you the whole armour of God, that ye may be able to withstand in the evil day, and having done all, to stand. Stand therefore, having your loins girt about*

with truth, and having on the breastplate of righteousness; And your feet shod with the preparation of the gospel of peace; Above all, taking the shield of faith, wherewith ye shall be able to quench all the fiery darts of the wicked. And take the helmet of salvation, and the sword of the Spirit, which is the word of God (Ephesians 6:13-17).

I want you to observe the instructions of the Spirit in the above verses. He instructs you to put on the whole armor of God. Notice He did not say some armor of God, but the whole. So, if you must survive and win spiritual warfare, you must put on the whole armor of God.

As a new believer, I used to use my imagination when reading this scripture. I would demonstrate placing on a helmet and shoes, breastplate and belt. I would also hold my Bible in my hand as if it were a sword and grab an imaginary shield to represent my faith. I think it quite childish, but necessary (smile). It makes sense when understanding the significance of being protected by armor divinely designed for you.

I had a friend that taught me about God's armor. I thought she was a bit dramatic until I felt the impressions of spiritual warfare. Having thoughts of suicide, foreboding joy, and unworthiness required spiritual intervention. God's Word replaced my worthless thoughts, faith removed the fear, and that Salvation Helmet and Righteousness Breastplate kept me alive. God knew that my life story was unique, but He used His armor to guard me, much like He is shielding you today.

Finally, the whole armor of God is not mysterious. God's armor is simple, effective weaponry that consists of truth, righteousness, producing peace with the gospel, faith, salvation and the Word of God.

Use God's armor as the Spirit prescribed and you will always win.

Truth *Belt (Girdle)- holds the armor together with the things that are true and without deception.*

Righteousness *Breastplate – God's approval and justification that protects vital organs, specifically the heart; and justice.*

Peace *shoes – ready to move and walk in the gospel of peace.*

Faith *Shield – the belief and trust in God, His word and His promises, used to "extinguish" your enemy's arrows.*

Salvation *Helmet – one's thoughts covered by the blood of Jesus as a professed believer in Christ, i.e., saved.*

Spirit *Sword – the Word of God, the Bible.*

Prayer

Dear Jesus, I know I am more than a conqueror and that the greater One lives in me. In the Name of Jesus Christ, I declare that I will always win in any spiritual warfare I encounter because I am equipped with the whole armor of God. Thank You for Your instructions in Jesus' Name I pray. Amen.

Day 1

What instructions have you received regarding spiritual warfare?

_____

_____

_____

_____

_____

_____

_____

_____

_____

_____

Day 2

What part of God's armor (truth belt, righteousness breastplate, peace shoes, faith shield, salvation helmet and Spirit sword) do you feel needs to be better developed in your life?

_____

_____

_____

_____

_____

_____

_____

_____

_____

_____

_____

Day 3

How can you put on the whole armor of God daily?

_____

_____

_____

_____

_____

_____

_____

_____

_____

_____

Day 4

What challenges do you feel hinder you from wearing the whole armor of God? How can you combat them?

_____

_____

_____

_____

_____

_____

_____

_____

_____

_____

Day 5

Write about a time when you saw someone else handle a terrible situation while wearing the whole armor of God. What was distinctive about their response to the situation?

_____

_____

_____

_____

_____

_____

_____

_____

_____

_____

Day 6

How does Ephesians 6:10-20 apply to current situations in your life?

_____

_____

_____

_____

_____

_____

_____

_____

_____

_____

_____

Day 7

What can you do TODAY to prepare for spiritual warfare?

_____

_____

_____

_____

_____

_____

_____

_____

_____

_____

Phase 4

Knowledge and Growth

[15] Wherefore I also, after I heard of your faith in the Lord Jesus, and love unto all the saints,[16] Cease not to give thanks for you, making mention of you in my prayers;[17] That the God of our Lord Jesus Christ, the Father of glory, may give unto you the spirit of wisdom and revelation in the knowledge of him:[18] The eyes of your understanding being enlightened; that ye may know what is the hope of his calling, and what the riches of the glory of his inheritance in the saints,[19] And what is the exceeding greatness of his power to us-ward who believe, according to the working of his mighty power,[20] Which he wrought in Christ, when he raised him from the dead, and set him at his own right hand in the heavenly places,[21] Far above all principality, and power, and might, and dominion, and every name that is named, not only in this world, but also in that which is to come:[22] And hath put all things under his feet, and gave him to be the head over all things to the church,[23] Which is his body, the fulness of him that filleth all in all (Ephesians 1:15-23). [14] For this cause I bow my knees unto the Father of our Lord Jesus Christ, [15] Of whom the whole family in heaven and earth is named, [16] That he would grant you, according to the riches of his glory, to be strengthened with might by his Spirit in the inner man; [17] That Christ may dwell in your hearts by faith; that ye, being rooted and grounded in love,[18] May be able to comprehend with all saints what is the breadth, and length, and depth, and height; [19] And to know the love of Christ, which passeth knowledge, that ye might be filled with

all the fulness of God. ²⁰ Now unto him that is able to do exceeding abundantly above all that we ask or think, according to the power that worketh in us, ²¹ Unto him be glory in the church by Christ Jesus throughout all ages, world without end. Amen (Ephesians 3:14-21).

But grow in grace, and in the knowledge of our Lord and Saviour Jesus Christ. To him be glory both now and for ever. Amen (2 Peter 3:18). Christian growth involves your development and increased knowledge of God and the Lord Jesus Christ. The more awareness of God you have, the better you can understand and serve Him. As a maturing believer, seeking knowledge of God activates blessings and enables you to operate in a higher grace, faith and glory than others.

Having limited knowledge about God, His promises and His will hinders your strength to produce at full capacity. What are you here for? Why did you experience trauma and pain in your life? What purpose does your life and testimony fulfill? You will never know until you know more about who God is, what He desires and how to access it.

God desires for you to progress as a Christian. It is not beneficial to settle as a babe after being saved because you will remain unskilled in the Way, Will and Word of righteousness. **For every one that useth milk is unskillful in the word of righteousness: for he is a babe** (Hebrews 5:13). It is babies that feed on milk. Just as babies grow to eat food with more substance, a Christian is also expected to increase spiritually and be entrusted with greater spiritual responsibilities.

As newborn babes, desire the sincere milk of the word, that ye may grow thereby; (1 Peter 2:2). One of the things you can do to increase in knowledge and grow as a Christian is to have a strong appetite for the Word of God. Cultivate the culture of daily studying the Word of God. Acquire a good daily devotional with a daily scripture reading plan. The Word of God says, "**to shew thyself approved unto God, a workman that needeth not to be ashamed, rightly dividing the word of truth** (2 Timothy 2:15). As you daily study the Word, you will inevitably become distinguished as the Berean Christians; they had an extended appetite for the Word. **Now the Berean Jews were of more noble character than those in Thessalonica, for they received the message with great eagerness and examined the Scriptures every day to see if what Paul said was true** (Acts 17:11, NIV).

The importance of the Word of God to your growth cannot be overemphasized. The Apostle Paul recognized this, hence he strongly recommended the Word. **And now, brethren, I commend you to God, and to the word of his grace, which is able to build you up, and to give you the inheritance among all them who are sanctified** (Acts 20:32).

Another thing to do to increase in knowledge and grow as a Christian is to develop a passionate attitude toward prayer, especially praying in the Holy Spirit. **Likewise the Spirit also helpeth our infirmities: for we know not what we should pray for as we ought: but the Spirit itself maketh intercession for us with groanings which cannot be uttered** (Romans 8:26). As you steadily spend quality time in prayer, you will quickly mature into a vibrant Christian. The Apostle Paul is an example of a Christian who through prayers and fellowship with the Holy Spirit grew very fast. In 1 Corinthians 14:18, he declared **I thank my God, I speak with tongues more than ye all**. He knew the importance of praying in the Holy Spirit.

Fellowshipping with other believers in church is yet another thing that will facilitate your growth and help you increase in the knowledge of God. The Spirit of God admonished us thus: *Not forsaking the assembling of ourselves together, as the manner of some is; but exhorting one another: and so much the more, as ye see the day approaching* (Hebrews 10:25).

Even being positioned in my church, I continue to have weeks that I do not desire to attend services. I will toss and turn in bed, consider house chores or projects I could work on, or plan for a day of play instead. At times, I will travel and miss the local church services in that week. Every single time I go through this slump ad absence, I get weak. My ability to fight off negativity lessens and I find myself being a grumpy person at work and home. Attending services and meetings supports our growth in the Word and service of God. There is so much to learn by connecting with other Believers.

Regular church attendance affords you the opportunities to experience God in His reality. You will hear testimonies of how God performed mighty miracles that will inspire you and build your faith. Furthermore, at church meetings, you will learn the undiluted Word of God; have the opportunity to praise and worship God with other believers; and also use your skills to serve God as well as experience and encounter God's presence, both visually and audibly.

Prayer

Father Lord God, I am so grateful to You for granting me the opportunities to increase in knowledge and to grow as a Christian. Lord, I pray that as I meditate on Your Word, you will reveal Your wisdom and knowledge. Fill me with Your fullness, and I will continually grow in grace and knowledge. Thank You, Father, in Jesus' Name. Amen.

Day 1

What is the hope of God's calling?

_____

_____

_____

_____

_____

_____

_____

_____

_____

_____

_____

Day 2

For believers, God grants grace, riches, and power. What misconceptions or mistruths do you need to release to receive all that God has for you?

_____

_____

_____

_____

_____

_____

_____

_____

_____

_____

_____

Day 3

What areas in your life does your "inner man" need to be strengthening?

_____

_____

_____

_____

_____

_____

_____

_____

_____

_____

Day 4

How do others know that Christ dwells in your heart and that you are filled with His love?

_____

_____

_____

_____

_____

_____

_____

_____

_____

_____

_____

Day 5

Write a prayer that you can memorize and say daily to increase your knowledge and growth?

_____

_____

_____

_____

_____

_____

_____

_____

_____

_____

Day 6

Ask a friend or loved one what changes have they noticed about you recently. Write responses below. Do you agree? Disagree? Why or why not?

_____

_____

_____

_____

_____

_____

_____

_____

_____

_____

Day 7

What will you do TODAY to improve your understanding of God's purpose and will for your life?

_____

_____

_____

_____

_____

_____

_____

_____

_____

_____

Phase 5

The Lord is Good

¹ It is a good thing to give thanks unto the LORD, and to sing praises unto thy name, O Most High: ² To shew forth thy lovingkindness in the morning, and thy faithfulness every night (Psalm 92:1-2).

O give thanks unto the LORD; for he is good; for his mercy endureth for ever (1Chronicles 16:34). Our text scripture instructs us to give thanks to the Lord because He is good and His love is everlasting. Johnson Oatman, the songwriter, wrote, "*Count your blessings, and name them one by one and it will surprise you what the Lord has done*" (1897). How true? If you are diligent enough to notice God's goodness towards you, your family, colleagues, and brethren in church, you will be filled with gratitude to the Lord always. Hallelujah!

All around us are pieces of evidence of God's goodness. From the air, we breathe; the sun and rains we enjoy; the fertile agricultural lands; the peace and prosperity in our country and the families He has given us. We have plenty of reasons to be thankful to God. On a personal level and as Christians, we cannot be grateful enough to God for sending the Lord Jesus Christ to die for our sins. In doing so, given us eternal life; His nature of righteousness; and the Holy Spirit. He answers our prayers, and we have the privilege to be called His sons. ***For the LORD God is a sun and shield: the LORD will give grace and glory: no good*** *thing will he withhold from them that walk uprightly* (Psalm 84:11).

Do not be ungrateful by refusing to acknowledge what the Lord has done for you. There are people whose perception towards life is to always find faults. They never see any good or recognize to be thankful to the Lord. To be grateful is to be deserving of more. Learn to appreciate God and to the people who God has used to bless you.

I will praise thee, O LORD, with my whole heart; I will shew forth all thy marvellous works (Psalm 9:1). One of the ways you can show gratitude to the Lord is in praise and worship. Learn to sing songs of praise to the Lord. Singing a song of praise to God is not about singing the correct key or melody as much as it is a joyful noise unto the Lord sang with a pure heart of gratitude. **A Psalm of praise. Make a joyful noise unto the LORD, all ye lands (**Psalm 100:1).

God loves music. The angels in heaven sing His praises daily. **And one cried unto another, and said, Holy, holy, holy, *is* the LORD of hosts: the whole earth *is* full of his glory** (Isaiah 6:3). With our voices, we can make a sound that lights up the heavens as it is holy and acceptable unto the Lord. Praise Him in song!

Dance. Move your body. You can bow down, lift your hands, clap your hands, step around in a circle, lay prostrate and even jump up and down all of which are moving or dancing in praise. Some are more skilled and can follow a choreographed routine in praise dance. Others step side-to-side and clap their hands. However, you move for the Lord, praise Him with your movement, dance. **Let them praise his name in the dance: let them sing praises unto him with the timbrel and harp** (Psalm 149:3).

With a heart of gratitude, worship Him in the beauty of holiness. *O worship the LORD in the beauty of holiness: fear before him, all the earth* (Psalm 96:9). Worshipping the Father is a testament of our intimacy with Him. To do so is to have knowledge of who God is, not only what He can do. Intimacy allows God to reveal himself to you as He delights Himself in you. God doesn't require a recipe or formula to prove Himself in your life. However, worship is what we do with Him.

Testify of His wondrous deeds so that men may know that the Lord is mighty in your midst. *Take with you words, and turn to the LORD: say to him, Take away all iniquity, and receive us graciously: so will we render the calves of our lips* (Hosea 14:2).

Furthermore, you can also show gratitude to the Lord by worshipping Him with your substances. Like David, learn to offer to God things that are most valuable to you. *And the king said to Araunah, Nay; but I will surely buy it of thee at a price: neither will I offer burnt offerings unto the LORD my God of that which dost cost me nothing. So David bought the threshingfloor and the oxen for fifty shekels of silver* (2 Samuel 24:24).

Prayer

Father God, thank You for Your loving kindness. Your wondrous deeds appear all around me as I see Your goodness and love demonstrated. I appreciate You for blessing me with grace and the good life. Daily You load me with benefits. Amen.

Day 1

How should you praise and thank God? (Hint: Psalm 92:1)

_____

_____

_____

_____

_____

_____

_____

_____

_____

_____

_____

Day 2

What will you do differently to express gratitude for the many blessings you have?

_____

_____

_____

_____

_____

_____

_____

_____

_____

_____

Day 3

How can you praise God without being embarrassed? Is there a place or time of day that feels more comfortable?

_____

_____

_____

_____

_____

_____

_____

_____

_____

_____

_____

Day 4

What can you do to increase your praise and faithfulness every day?

_____

_____

_____

_____

_____

_____

_____

_____

_____

_____

Day 5

Think of songs you've heard that express praise and thanksgiving. Write your hymn or poem (words of thankfulness) for God's wondrous acts.

_____

_____

_____

_____

_____

_____

_____

_____

_____

_____

Day 6

When is it a good time to dance?

_____

_____

_____

_____

_____

_____

_____

_____

_____

_____

Day 7

What can you do daily to build your relationship with God?

_____

_____

_____

_____

_____

_____

_____

_____

_____

_____

Phase 6

Unity of the Spirit

¹ I therefore, the prisoner of the Lord, beseech you that ye walk worthy of the vocation wherewith ye are called, ² With all lowliness and meekness, with longsuffering, forbearing one another in love; ³ Endeavouring to keep the unity of the Spirit in the bond of peace. ⁴ There is one body, and one Spirit, even as ye are called in one hope of your calling; ⁵ One Lord, one faith, one baptism, ⁶ One God and Father of all, who is above all, and through all, and in you all (Ephesians 4:1-6).

And all those who had believed were together and had all things in common; and they began selling their property and possessions and were sharing them with all, as anyone might have need (Acts 2:44-45, NASB). Never find yourself feeling alone or act as though you are alone. The Word of God says, **No, you have come to Mount Zion, to the city of the living God, the heavenly Jerusalem, and to countless thousands of angels in a joyful gathering. You have come to the assembly of God's firstborn children, whose names are written in heaven. You have come to God himself, who is the judge over all things. You have come to the spirits of the righteous ones in heaven who have now been made perfect** (Hebrews 12:22-23, NLT). Can you see that? As far as God is concerned, you are always in the exceptional and exciting company of angels and spirits of just men made perfect.

One of the devil's strategies is to make us feel lonely and alone because of his intention to destroy. If he can make you believe this lie, he will then begin to attack your mind with thoughts of being abandoned, ashamed, and not good enough. Before long, depression and pity will set in and be the death of your spiritual life and connection to God and other believers.

The Lord Jesus Christ promised to always be with you. "*...lo, I am with you alway, even unto the end of the world. Amen*" (Matthew 28:20 b.). For this reason, replace that feeling of self-pity, shame, not good enough and guilt that the devil has sold to you. No matter how correct or seemingly good enough your reason to always be by yourself, it is not compelling enough. The Psalmist said, "*... Behold, how good and how pleasant it is for brethren to dwell together in unity*" (Psalm 133:1).

God wants you to form unified bonds with others in the church. The only group the Lord forbids you to associate with are sinners. *Be ye not unequally yoked together with unbelievers: for what fellowship hath righteousness with unrighteousness? And what communion hath light with darkness? And what concord (harmony) hath Christ with Belial? or what part hath he that believeth with an infidel?* (2 Corinthians 6:14-15). Your brothers and sisters in the church are not infidels, but saints. Forthwith, you are permitted to associate with them.

It took more than church attendance for me to realize my wrong patterns of thinking; it took a connection of assembling with Believers on a consistent basis. I was challenged in conversation causing me to consider deeply my motives and compare them to the Word. I recall telling a fellow believer of all the 'sacrifices' I made to demonstrate my Christianity such as maintaining sobriety, vowing to celibacy, and removing myself from invalidating and sinful activities. I concluded my conversation with, "God better bless me." This statement prompted a discussion about my motivation and entitlement. I was surprised to learn that while I had spent most of my time in study and attending church services, I had impure motives and felt entitled. Relating with those who believed in Christ Jesus as I did, encouraged growth and deeper levels of healing from my past. You must connect!

Apart from the blessings the Lord gives when you fellowship with believers under a corporate anointing, being involved in the church gives you the opportunity to bless God with your talents. Being in oneness encourages experiential learning. As angels sang and defended God' people, likewise are we to 'do' something other than warm the seats of the congregation halls. If you can sing or usher, you can join the choir or ushering department and become useful there. The Lord desires you to activate your gifts among brethren and in the church. To act otherwise is discriminatory or prideful. Race, sex, and status notwithstanding, <u>we are all one in Christ</u>. ***There is*** *neither Jew nor Greek, there is neither bond nor free, there is neither male nor female: for ye are all one in Christ Jesus* (Galatians 3:28). Therefore, demonstrate the unity of the Spirit by attending and participating in Christian activities and commit to being involved so that God can use you and help you fulfill your destiny in Christ.

Prayer

Father, thank You for teaching me Your Word today on the importance of being involved in church. I realize that I am not alone, but I am always in the company of angels, the Holy Spirit and the Lord Jesus Christ. In Christ, I live, move and have my being. I refuse to allow the devil to lie to me or cause me to disassociate from the godly company You have created for me. I commit to connect and stay connected with the harmonious group devoted to you. Thank You, Lord, in Jesus' Name I pray. Amen.

Day 1

How can you get connected to the Body of Christ, amongst Believers and godly people?

_____

_____

_____

_____

_____

_____

_____

_____

_____

_____

Day 2

What fears and concerns do you have in joining small groups at your local church?

Day 3

How can you overcome those fears?

_____

_____

_____

_____

_____

_____

_____

_____

_____

_____

Day 4

What scriptures in the Bible speak directly to your inhibitions and fears?

_____

_____

_____

_____

_____

_____

_____

_____

_____

_____

Day 5

How can you use those scriptures when meeting new people?

_____

_____

_____

_____

_____

_____

_____

_____

_____

_____

Day 6

What can you do to increase your participation with Believers who look, act and worship differently than you?

_____

_____

_____

_____

_____

_____

_____

_____

_____

_____

Day 7

Separation and isolation are issues in our community. What will you begin to do to build unity amongst the diversity of Believers?

_____

_____

_____

_____

_____

_____

_____

_____

_____

Phase 7

Rejoice and Think

⁴ Rejoice in the Lord always: and again I say, Rejoice. ⁵ Let your moderation be known unto all men. The Lord is at hand. ⁶ Be careful for nothing; but in every thing by prayer and supplication with thanksgiving let your requests be made known unto God. ⁷ And the peace of God, which passeth all understanding, shall keep your hearts and minds through Christ Jesus. ⁸ Finally, brethren, whatsoever things are true, whatsoever things are honest, whatsoever things are just, whatsoever things are pure, whatsoever things are lovely, whatsoever things are of good report; if there be any virtue, and if there be any praise, think on these things (Philippians 4:4-8).

Rejoice in the Lord always: and again I will say, Rejoice *(*Philippians 4:4). All around us are circumstances to make us anxious. As you turn on your television or radio, the only news you hear are those that can cause your heart to fail. You listen to a broadcast of global economic meltdown, unemployment, impoverished little children abused, terrorists' attacks, earthquakes, shootings, sex trafficking, murder, etc. However, the Lord's admonition to us is for us not to be anxious. ***Be careful for nothing; but in every thing by prayer and***

supplication with thanksgiving let your requests be made known unto God (Philippians 4:6). When you learn to take every concern to the Lord in prayer, the peace of God, which exceeds the understanding of man, guards, protects and barricades your hearts and minds through Christ Jesus. This level of promise is reason enough to rejoice always.

Life is praiseworthy. Your life is praiseworthy. Life experiences have enabled you to endure heartaches and pains that some may account as unbearable or unbelievable. You serve an incredible way making God who ensures that your treacherous journey leads to Him, laced with joy and thanksgiving. Having endured disappointments in my life, I could have given up on life altogether. There were times when I became suicidal and wanted to end my life. God knew I would have days like that. He put people, scripture, and angels in place to counter those deceitful and destructive ideas. God knew you would think of yourself as unworthy of life with thoughts of bitterness and discouragement.

God is the all-knowing Creator, Elohim. He inspired the words of this scripture to keep our mind on Him. Those things, whether life circumstances, financial, relationship or family, are to be wrapped in the reality of who God is and not in how you feel about them. What does that mean? I asked the same question. It proposes that having family issues is not an overwhelming negative feeling of disgust but a light of hope that no matter how painful relationships get and opinions vary, you love each other. Your thoughts about your family are to remain the same loving and accepting thoughts before arguments, disagreements or decisions because that is TRUE, you love each other.

Similarly, what is "...**honest, just, pure, lovely, and of good report**..." are to engulf your thoughts about every aspect of the world you experience and live. In your life, you gain poverty form worrying, not prosperity. *Who of you by worrying can add a single hour to your life?* (Luke 12:25, NIV). Yes, it costs you significantly to worry about things you cannot change and have no control over. Instead, smile and rejoice as the situation could always be worse than it appears. All you have to do is release your desire and tell God all about it and celebrate. Hallelujah!

Caution is required when the devil tries to attack your heart with wrong thoughts, deliberately refuse him. **Tell your mind how and what to think**. Remember, your thoughts are subjected to your authority to command them. You can renew your mind to think of pleasant images at any time. *Be not deceived: evil communications corrupt good manners* (1Corinthians 15:33). Pay attention to the things you dwell on. If you keep filling your mind with things that bring in fear, doubt, weakness, and sickness, you will be in violation of God's command to rejoice and think about what He has perfected and provided for you.

You must be mindful of the programs you watch on television and the internet; the contents you read in books and magazines or listen to through the radio.

Likewise, be careful of the friends you keep and the places you frequent. What you surround yourself with will impact your thoughts and opinions. Ask God to remove things in your life that do not please Him. He will. Ask God to replace and renew your thoughts. He will show you how. Ask God to bring you clean entertainment, something that makes you rejoice. He will.

Prayer

Thank You, Heavenly Father for the impact of Your Word on my mind. My heart and mind are consumed with Your peace that surpasses all understanding. I refuse to be anxious and worry about anything. Instead, with prayers and supplications, I will always make my request known to You. I declare that my mind stays on You through Your Word. Thank You, Holy Father, in Jesus' Name. Amen.

Day 1

Write a list of things, people or situations you worry about (things troubling to your spirit or that may be negative or taxing to your life).

_____

_____

_____

_____

_____

_____

_____

_____

_____

_____

Day 2

What can you do in prayer and supplication to embrace God's peace about your list from Day 1?

_____

_____

_____

_____

_____

_____

_____

_____

_____

_____

Day 3

What prevents you from letting go of your concerns, worries, and anxieties?

_____

_____

_____

_____

_____

_____

_____

_____

_____

_____

Day 4

Which thought command (true, honest, just, pure, lovely, and of good report) can you apply to what worries you?

_____

_____

_____

_____

_____

_____

_____

_____

_____

_____

Day 5

Write a prayer that addresses your fears, doubts or anxieties in 3-5 sentences.

_____

_____

_____

_____

_____

_____

_____

_____

_____

_____

Day 6

What can you do to Rejoice and Think better about your situation(s)?

_____

_____

_____

_____

_____

_____

_____

_____

_____

_____

Day 7

Today, I commit myself before God that I will no longer worry about _____. I will speak
(worry/fear/doubt)
the Word of God and think on the things that are
True, Honest, Just, Pure, Lovely and of Good Report.

_____

_____

_____

_____

_____

_____

_____

_____

_____

Phase 8

The Believer's Duty

¹ I beseech you therefore, brethren, by the mercies of God, that ye present your bodies a living sacrifice, holy, acceptable unto God, which is your reasonable service.² And be not conformed to this world: but be ye transformed by the renewing of your mind, that ye may prove what is that good, and acceptable, and perfect, will of God (Romans 12:1-2).

And be not conformed to this world: but be ye transformed by the renewing of your mind, that ye may prove what is that good, and acceptable, and perfect, will of God (Romans 12:2). One sure way you can deal with shame, guilt, fear, and pride is to renew your mind with the Word; see yourself in the light of the Word of God. If you do not stimulate your mind with the Word of God, the devil will take advantage of you. This lack is evident by those who suffer from shame, pride, and guilt, and commit suicide or never blossom from childhood abuse or never develop beyond a traumatic experience. They allow the devil to play tricks with their minds and only see condemnation and rejection, not even able to imagine God's mercies. **There is therefore now no condemnation to them which are in Christ Jesus, who walk not after the flesh, but after the Spirit** (Romans 8:1). You are in Christ, and you are free from condemnation, NOW!

As a Believer, realize you are not your past. In fact, you are bigger and better than your past experiences. Thus, do not allow your past mistakes to define you. The Word of God says, **Therefore if any man be in Christ, he is a new creature: old things are passed away; behold, all things are become new** (2 Corinthians 5:17). You are in Christ now, and your past is gone. You are a renewed living being; your life is made new. Glory to God!

Anytime the devil or anyone tries to link you to your past refuse it. Even a mistake made after becoming a Christian, if you have asked God to forgive you, obtain forgiveness and move on. Your Heavenly Father has forgiven you and has no record of that wrong with Him. **If we confess our sins, he is faithful and just to forgive us our sins, and to cleanse us from all unrighteousness** (1 John 1:9).

Sometimes some of us tend to be more serious or righteous than God Himself. Even after we have asked the Lord for forgiveness, we keep dwelling on the mistake and allowing our thoughts to continue condemning us, magnifying the wrong more than the mercies of God. This dwelling place is a form of **pride**, and it is very **wrong**. God is higher than your opinions. If He did not condemn you, you do not have the right to condemn yourself nor allow your thoughts to convict you. **Even if our heart (conscience) condemn us, God is greater than our heart (conscience), and knoweth all things** (1 John 3:20).

Study to shew thyself approved unto God, a workman that needeth not to be ashamed, rightly

dividing the word of truth (2 Timothy 2:15). You must, therefore, delight yourself in the Word so that you know your inheritance in Christ Jesus and be able to call yourself what God has named you. This awareness will remove shame from your path and make you see yourself as God has made you. ***But ye are a chosen generation, a royal priesthood, an holy nation, a peculiar people;*** *that ye should shew forth the praises of him who hath called you out of darkness into his marvellous light* (1 Peter 2:9). Henceforth, this is how you should see yourself because this is how God sees you.

Prayer

Father and LORD, My God, thank You for the identity You have given me in Christ. Henceforth, this is the only way I see myself. I refuse to allow the devil to play his pranks on me again, making me feel worthless, guilty, shameful, prideful, and fearful. Your Word has shown me that You chose me, royal, holy, and peculiar. In that, I embrace, own and appreciate as I am in Your marvelous light. Glory to Your Name forever more. In Jesus' Name, I pray. Amen.

Day 1

Who did God call you to be? What name(s) did He give you?

_____

_____

_____

_____

_____

_____

_____

_____

_____

Day 2

What does it mean to be _____?
(what God called you)

_____

_____

_____

_____

_____

_____

_____

_____

_____

_____

Day 3

What can you do to release the desire to conform in your family, home, school, church, community, work, etc.?

_____

_____

_____

_____

_____

_____

_____

_____

_____

_____

Day 4

What will you do to renew your mind daily?

_____

_____

_____

_____

_____

_____

_____

_____

_____

_____

Day 5

What is your duty as a Believer? (Hint: Romans 12:1-2)

_____

_____

_____

_____

_____

_____

_____

_____

_____

_____

Day 6

What can you do to present your body as a living sacrifice that is _holy and acceptable_ to God?

_____

_____

_____

_____

_____

_____

_____

_____

_____

Day 7

What scripture will you read <u>daily</u> to be transformed by the renewing of your mind?

_____

_____

_____

_____

_____

_____

_____

_____

_____

_____

Phase 9

Conqueror's Believe

28 And we know that all things work together for good to them that love God, to them who are the called according to his purpose....30 Moreover whom he did predestinate, them he also called: and whom he called, them he also justified: and whom he justified, them he also glorified. 31 What shall we then say to these things? If God be for us, who can be against us?... 35 Who shall separate us from the love of Christ? shall tribulation, or distress, or persecution, or famine, or nakedness, or peril, or sword? 36 As it is written, For thy sake we are killed all the day long; we are accounted as sheep for the slaughter. 37 Nay, in all these things we are more than conquerors through him that loved us. 38 For I am persuaded, that neither death, nor life, nor angels, nor principalities, nor powers, nor things present, nor things to come, 39 Nor height, nor depth, nor any other creature, shall be able to separate us from the love of God, which is in Christ Jesus our Lord (Romans 8:28, 30-31, 35-39).

Nay, in all these things we are <u>more than conquerors</u> through him that loved us (Romans 8:37). Focus on the underlined phrase in verse, **<u>more than conquerors</u>**. The Spirit of God says we are 'more than conquerors' and not that 'we are GOING to conquer.' There is a big difference between the two phrases. More than a conqueror means you have been declared a conqueror before you even start. The Greek translation makes it clear that you are "**completely and overwhelmingly victorious**" (HELPS Word Study). This predisposition is not to your efforts, but through Him that loved you. Hallelujah!

Without the awareness of who God says we are, we fail to walk uprightly, we fail to demonstrate God's glory in the earth, and we fail to be examples of God's love to those who do and do not believe. Our testimony speaks volumes of who God is, and how he manifests His word and love in the earth. Talking and thinking of ourselves as defeated is contrary to what God has ordained for us. The love of God is so perfect that in every fruitless, complicated, and adverse situation He has made us victorious.

In recollection of my walk with God, I faced unemployment. I had sent out numerous applications to every position I qualified for to secure employment. As a single parent, work is critical. I began interviewing for positions I was overqualified for and positions where I was perfectly qualified. Job after job, the letter came in the mailbox with the words you hate to see when in need of employment, "sorry, but…" Rent was due, and all other bills were delinquent. My heart desired a specific position, I applied for and conducted an excellent interview but was not selected. Knowing my qualifications and fed up with rejection, I called the decision makers requesting feedback. In a matter of months, I was called back for another interview and offered the position as well as another high paying position with another company in the same week. While I could have been filled with doubt, packed my bags and gave up, instead I remained faithful. I knew above all else, that God had an employment position perfectly designed just for me, and He did. The job I accepted allowed me to gain invaluable professional training that expanded my career and skills. I never saw myself less than victorious. I was bold enough to believe God for the job I wrote out on my vision board. And God blessed me with what I had requested.

As far as God is concerned, you are completely and overwhelmingly victorious, more than a conqueror, because He made you so. **But thanks be to God, which giveth us the victory through our Lord Jesus Christ** (1 Corinthians 15:57). These facts align you with your inheritance in Christ Jesus. God has already given you the victory through the Lord Jesus Christ. Note the verb tenses used here. He already pre-orchestrated and predestined your advantage in every situation you can imagine. What God expects from you is to walk in the revelation of what He has already done for you, 'more than a conqueror.' It is already done!

As a child of God, it will be a demonstration of faithlessness if you play the victim's role. Remember, He made you victorious and not a victim. According to the Word of God, anyone that is born of God has overcome this world and all of its' challenges. **For whatsoever is born of God overcometh the world: and this is the victory that overcometh the world, even our faith** (1 John 5:4). It is your faith in the Lord

Jesus Christ and His finished works that have given you the victory. So never allow the devil or the circumstances of life beat you down.

Of course, you are going to face diverse challenges and trials. Instead of getting discouraged or discomfited, see with the eyes of the victor that you are. See the sufferings as opportunities for you to activate and demonstrate your faith; to prove to the devil that you are born of God. *I have told you all this so that you may have peace in me. Here on earth you will have many trials and sorrows. But take heart, because I have overcome the world* (John 16:33, NLT).

Remember that no challenge or trial is strong enough to pull you down if you do not allow it. *Who shall separate us from the love of Christ? shall tribulation, or distress, or persecution, or famine, or nakedness, or peril, or sword?* (Romans 8:35). Keep seeing yourself as a victor, more than a conqueror, and you will always win in life. Praise God!

Prayer

Precious Father, I thank You today for the victory You have given me. I declare by the authority of the Holy Spirit that I daily walk in the perpetual victory, demonstrate Your power and grace, and declare that no weapon formed against me will prosper and every tongue that rises against me, I condemn in the Name of the Lord Jesus Christ. Amen.

Day 1

What prevents you from embracing faith as a conqueror and from releasing the fear of unbelief?

_____

_____

_____

_____

_____

_____

_____

_____

_____

_____

Day 2

Write a list of hopeful, victorious thoughts.

_____

_____

_____

_____

_____

_____

_____

_____

_____

_____

_____

Day 3

Give an example of when a bad situation turned out to your benefit.

_____

_____

_____

_____

_____

_____

_____

_____

_____

Day 4

How has trouble, internal pressure, affliction, and persecution separated you from Christ's love?

_____

_____

_____

_____

_____

_____

_____

_____

_____

_____

Day 5

What does being more than a conqueror mean to YOU?

_____

_____

_____

_____

_____

_____

_____

_____

_____

_____

Day 6

What does it mean for you to be predestinated, called, justified, and glorified? (Hint: Romans 8:30)

_____

_____

_____

_____

_____

_____

_____

_____

_____

_____

Day 7

How will you trust God and build your faith to defeat negative thoughts and overcome difficult situations?

_____

_____

_____

_____

_____

_____

_____

_____

_____

_____

Phase 10

Spiritual Authority

4 (For the weapons of our warfare are not carnal, but mighty through God to the pulling down of strong holds;) 5 Casting down imaginations, and every high thing that exalteth itself against the knowledge of God, and bringing into captivity every thought to the obedience of Christ;(2 Corinthians 10:4-5).

Behold, I give unto you power to tread on serpents and scorpions, and over all the power of the enemy: and nothing shall by any means hurt you (Luke 10:19). Spiritual power and authority received from the Lord is the dynamic ability to effect changes anywhere you want. However, there are some Christians in whom this power is dormant. Lack of influence is evident when you are unaware, inactive due to fear, sin or taught incorrectly. For you to start using your power, you have to stir it aflame by praying fervently in other tongues. As you pray in the Holy Spirit, that power in you will be activated for you to use anytime. Having the accurate knowledge of God's Word will enhance your ability to use your spiritual authority. It will eliminate condemnations and guilt from your mind and give you boldness to activate and exercise your authority. It is time for you to walk in the experiential explosion of God's dynamic power.

The authority you have from the Lord transcends the natural realm to the supernatural realm. In other words, you can exercise this authority both in the physical and spiritual spheres. You can cast out devils, heal the sick, raise the dead, stop the sun in its course, command blessings and even forgive sins (Matthew 10:8). The Word of God says concerning you: ***Herein is our love made perfect, that we may have boldness in the day of judgment: because <u>as he is, so are we in this world</u>*** (1John 4:17). The underlined phrase shows you who you are. As the Lord Jesus Christ is in heaven presently, that is how you are in this world. The same way He demonstrated the power of God, that is the same way God expects you to put your authority to work and pull-down strongholds. Exercising your authority, you will recognize that the adversaries are not humans even though they appear as humans. You adversaries are the devil, evil spirits and those things that align with the Anti-Christ. It is the devil that instigates people to hate, harm, and plan evil against you. Therefore, when executing your spiritual authority, focus on the devil and his demons, not your brothers and sisters. Declare with boldness and in faith what you want, and they will oblige. ***Submit yourselves therefore to God. <u>Resist the devil, and he will flee from you</u>*** (James 4:7).

As a child, I wanted to be a boy. Boys seemed to get more attention than me, the girl. There were times when I looked in the mirror and saw more masculine characteristics than female images. Having broad shoulders, I would grunt like the animated character Incredible Hulk©. Around my neck and shoulders, I looked like a fullback on an American football team. The desire to be a boy was perpetuated in my young adult life as I witnessed male privilege and women's denial of access. I hated being a woman and all of the limitations associated with being of the inferior being.

*By reading the Daily Journey Devotion, God exposed His truth about me, as a woman. I found an appreciation for God's perfect will make me a woman. He shared His word and promise "...**for I am fearfully and wonderfully made...**" (Psalm 139:14) "...**after our likeness... in his own image...**" (Genesis 1:26-27). God made it clear to me that "...**What God hath cleansed, that call not thou common**" (Acts 10:15).*

God has purpose and promise specifically for His women as validated in the stories of Jael (Judges 4:21), "Deborah (Judges 4:4), Rahab (Joshua 6:25), Esther (book of Esther), Ruth (book of Ruth), and Mary the mother of Jesus" (Nelson, 2017). Through the devotional process, the imagination and misguidance of my youth were 'pulled down' out of my head as a fundamental belief. Those thoughts were against Christ. They had to be 'cast out' in God's loving way.

<u>But ye shall receive power, after the Holy Ghost is come upon you:</u> and ye shall be witnesses unto me both in Jerusalem, and in all Judea, and in Samaria, and unto the uttermost part of the earth (Acts 1:8). Notice that the Lord gave every Christian this authority. If you have received the Lord Jesus as Lord and Savior of your life and you have also received the Holy Spirit, you have this power. You can lay hands on the sick, and they will recover; you can cast out devils and raise the dead. Halleluiah!

Prayer

Dear Lord God, thank You for the authority I have received of the Lord Jesus Christ. I exercise it with boldness and in faith. I use the power to effect changes in my home, family, workplace, community, church, and region to the Glory of God. As I lay my hands on the sick, they recover expeditiously. The dead are resuscitated back to life as I exercise your Holy given power. I am rebirthed with your authority in mind, body, and soul to set captives free, in Jesus' Name, Amen.

Day 1

What prevents you from activating the God-given authority to do greater works than Jesus did when He walked the earth?

_____

_____

_____

_____

_____

_____

_____

_____

_____

_____

Day 2

What imaginations, thoughts or beliefs do you have that go against a precept or principle found in the Bible? Don't be embarrassed, list them all.

_____

_____

_____

_____

_____

_____

_____

_____

_____

_____

_____

Day 3

Which Bible verses counter five (5) items on your list from Day 2? Write them below.

_____

_____

_____

_____

_____

_____

_____

_____

_____

_____

Day 4

With your God-given power, how will you cast down imaginations and thoughts of things that go against Christ?

_____

_____

_____

_____

_____

_____

_____

_____

_____

_____

Day 5

What thoughts do you need to capture and destroy to reach your destiny? In other words, what do you think that demotes you rather than promotes you?

_____

_____

_____

_____

_____

_____

_____

_____

_____

Day 6

Read 2 Corinthians 10:4-5 three (3) times, then write spiritual impressions and prophetic utterances God has given you about this scripture.

_____

_____

_____

_____

_____

_____

_____

_____

_____

_____

Day 7

Write your strength mantra (an affirming statement that you repeat often) or affirmation with abbreviated scriptures.

Example:
My strength mantra: *I am fearfully and wonderfully made, in His image and likeness. I am predestined for greatness, blessed and highly favored among women. I have strength in God and from God that is inseparable by anything man tries to do. I am more than a conqueror through Christ, who loves me.*

<u>My Personal Strength Mantra</u>

_____

_____

_____

_____

_____

_____

Phase 11

Christian Virtues

12 Put on therefore, as the elect of God, holy and beloved, bowels of mercies, kindness, humbleness of mind, meekness, longsuffering;13 Forbearing one another, and forgiving one another, if any man have a quarrel against any: even as Christ forgave you, so also do ye.14 And above all these things put on charity, which is the bond of perfectness. 15 And let the peace of God rule in your hearts, to the which also ye are called in one body; and be ye thankful (Colossians 3:12-15).

And let the peace of God rule in your hearts, to which also ye are called in one body; and be ye thankful (Colossians 3:12–15). The Word of God is manifest, **Therefore, if any man be in Christ, he is a new creature: old things are passed away; behold, all things are become new** (2Corinthians 5:17). Probably before you were born again you were very temperamental, impatient, and proud. Now that you are a member of the Body of Christ and filled with the Holy Spirit, you need to prayerfully put off your old self and put on the renewed man after God. **And have put on the new man, which is renewed in knowledge after the image of him that created him** (Colossians 3:10).

Christian virtues are qualities you must exhibit as a Christian that will make others know who you truly say you are – a Christian. From the scripture above, we can surely identify these virtues. They include mercies or compassion; kindness; humbleness of mind or humility; meekness or gentleness; and longsuffering or patience. Other attributes include being peaceful, loving and being thankful.

When you learn to display these virtues, you will avert a lot of problems and troubles. Instead of being temperamental or impatient, the Spirit of God will help you become humble, patient, gentle, thankful, peaceful and loving. These were the qualities the Lord Jesus Christ exhibited that made Him succeed in ministry. The scripture records that though He was not guilty of sin or any wrongdoing, He humbled Himself to death on the cross. ***And being found in fashion as a man, he humbled himself, and became obedient* unto death, even *the* death *of the* cross** (Philippians 2:8).

Apart from prayers, submission to authority and studying the Word of God will also help you develop and exhibit these virtues. As you explore the Word, the Spirit of God will open the eyes of your understanding to know the areas in your life where you need to make adjustments. Even though I had been a publicly professed believer, I had some challenges looking and sounding like a Believer. Not only did I have an issue with profanity, but I also held grudges against those whom I considered untrustworthy or deceitful. Submitting to leadership was easy because they didn't hear me curse when I was angry or upset. They also didn't know I disliked working with deceptive people. However, when instructed or suggested to complete an assignment with my coworkers, I did it and never shared public disgust.

However, I was displeasing God. Why? Because my heart wasn't right. Even though you obey, if your real motives are not pure then your submission is deceptive and unacceptable to God. God told us to do things as if we are doing them for Him. Likewise, He told us to abide by those who ruled over us. Any time a boss or superior gives you an instruction, you must obey with humility, not pride. God does not appreciate our disrespect to authority nor does he applaud our obedience when enacted in arrogance or self-righteousness. Our submission reveals our character.

Submitting to authority can influence you and cause you to improve your character. As you practice humility and submission, others will notice the change in you. Remember that your character defines you; it brings out the contents that are inside of you. Therefore, dutifully covet these virtues and use them to align your life with the Word.

Prayer

Most Gracious and Heavenly Father, be exalted and magnified. Your Word has brought me an understanding on how I can become better. Lord, by the power of the Holy Spirit, I declare that I will dutifully covet these virtues, practice submission and humility so that I can be obedient to Your will and be transformed into the image You desire of me. Thank You, Lord for teaching me your virtues, in Jesus' Name. Amen.

Day 1

Remember a time when you were mean, unloving or impatient. Write a list of words that described how you treated others and responded to situations.

_____

_____

_____

_____

_____

_____

_____

_____

_____

_____

_____

Day 2

Of the Christian virtues listed in Colossians 3:12-15, which of them do you find lacking in your character?

_____

_____

_____

_____

_____

_____

_____

_____

_____

_____

Day 3

List people who have hurt you and offenses that have been devoted toward you. Place them in order from most significant to least painful.

_____

_____

_____

_____

_____

_____

_____

_____

_____

_____

Day 4

What will it take for you to forbear, forgive and love those who have hurt you the most?

_____

_____

_____

_____

_____

_____

_____

_____

_____

_____

Day 5

From your list of people who have offended or hurt you, write out who you will forgive, who you will love past the hurt, and who you will forbear in spite of the pain. Make the commitment to forgive them in the next seven (7) days.

_____

_____

_____

_____

_____

_____

_____

_____

_____

_____

_____

Day 6

God requires submission, in heart and action. How can you submit to your employer, spouse, parents, leader and authority figure?

_____

_____

_____

_____

_____

_____

_____

_____

_____

_____

Day 7

What virtue(s) will you work on to improve your character?

_____

_____

_____

_____

_____

_____

_____

_____

_____

_____

_____

Phase 12

Growing On

And because ye are sons, God hath sent forth the Spirit of his Son into your hearts, crying, Abba, Father (Galatians 4:6).

All scripture is given by inspiration of God, and is profitable for doctrine, for reproof, for correction, for instruction in righteousness: That the man of God may be perfect, throughly furnished unto all good works (2 Timothy 3:16-17). The inspiration of God gives scripture. The Holy Spirit inspired men of God to write the scriptures. All of the content of the Bible is not all the words of God. The Bible also contains the words of men, angels, kings, the devil, demons, and animals. However, as you determine to study the Bible, the Spirit of God will guide you to know the contents that exist solely by the Spirit of God and not as exemplified by others.

Everything you need to live the good life in Christ is wrapped in the Word of God. There is not a subject or any issue in life that the Word of God did not talk about. In fact, all human endeavors have at least a scripture or two addressing them respectively.

Again, a careful study of the scriptures will show you the characteristics of the Holy Scripture and what the Lord God designed it to achieve. The scriptures are profitable *for doctrine,* **for reproof, for correction, for instruction in righteousness**. HELPS Word-studies defines the four (4) essential principles of this scripture from Greek translation and interpretation as:

Doctrine (didaskalia, #1319) – "Applied-teaching; Christian doctrine (teaching) as it especially extends to its necessary lifestyle (applications)."

Reproof (elegchos, #1650) – "Inner conviction focuses on God confirming His inbirthing of faith ("the internal persuasion from Him.")."

Correction (epanorthósis, #1882) – "Suitable because straight, i.e. restored to its (original) proper condition; hence correction (referring to something that is aptly "straightened out")."

Instruction (paideia, #3809) – "Instruction that trains someone to reach full development (maturity)."

The purpose is that you **may be perfect and equipped** to do all that God has designed and desired you to do. God wants you to have a lifestyle with evidence that you are His and exemplifies your reformation and maturity. Hallelujah!

If you abide in me, and my words abide in you, ye shall ask what ye will, and it shall be done unto you (John 15:7).

It is very crucial you have your private copy of the Bible so that you can easily have access to it, whether in print or electronically. There are several hardcopy versions of the Bible, electronic and online daily devotionals with good Bible study plans that will guide you to study the entire Bible in a year or two. Also, there are study and reference Bibles as well as other books designed for exploration of the scripture in your local bookstore or online.

Also, 'study' and not just read your Bible. Reading the Bible is a good start in your Christian walk. It allows you to become familiar with God and His promises and expectations. However, when you study the Bible, you begin to learn more about God's way and God's will for your healing, restoration, and purpose. Studying the Bible should include a concordance to translate and interpret the words used in the Bible so that you gain the most authentic message. While investigating, God will expose profound revelation, spiritual mysteries and intelligent application that will **build you up** and expand your knowledge while discovering your inheritance in Christ Jesus. *And now, brethren, I commend you to God, and to the word of his grace, which is able to build you up, and to give you an inheritance among all them which are sanctified* (Acts 20:32). The difference between reading and studying the Bible is asking questions. While you read the scriptures, you will have issues that will guide your study. Grow on!

Growing in Christ is reading, studying and applying the Word of God in your daily thoughts and actions. Once you have studied or heard a scripture, make it fit in your life. Do you need an answer to anything in life? Go to the Word. *Work hard so you can present yourself to God and receive his approval. Be a good worker, one who does not need to be ashamed and who correctly explains the word of truth* (2 Timothy 2:15). The key is that you study to know the truth for yourself and can share the gospel of Jesus with others.

God's word is relevant, revelatory, and releasing. Welcome Holy Spirit to revitalize your thirst for righteousness. The assistance of Holy Spirit in your studies to understand the scriptures cannot be overemphasized. Sincerely ask Him to guide you as you embrace the Word of God. Let Holy Spirit open your eyes of understanding as the sons of God.

NOTE: If you recently accepted Christ as your Savior and you desire to know more about Him, the Holy Spirit, and your salvation, many scholars suggest you begin with the gospel of Saint John. This chapter of the New Testament is easy to understand because it explains the ministry of Jesus Christ in plain language. You may also begin with the Book of Psalms which is full of promises and encouragement. As newborn babes, desire the sincere milk of the word, that ye may grow thereby (1 Peter 2:2).

Prayer

Precious Father, the very essence of Your Word *brings light; it gives understanding to the simple. Your Word came to build me up and show me my inheritance among them that are sanctified and holy. Lord, I declare that by the guidance of Your Spirit, I will daily study Your Word, praise and worship You and pray Your will be done on earth as it is in heaven. I realize that all that I ever need in life is wrapped up in the Word. Let the unction of the Holy Spirit minister to me as I grow on. Let teachers, mentors, and prophets speak and confirm Your Word in my life. Help me to understand Your mysteries and the essence of who You are. I declare that I am Yours as You are mine and I commit to follow You, proclaiming Your manifested glory by the blood of Jesus. Thank You, Father God, in Jesus' Name. Amen.*

Day 1

What tools do you need to acquire (or already have) in addition to a Bible to study, translate and interpret the Word of God?

_____

_____

_____

_____

_____

_____

_____

_____

_____

_____

Day 2

What have you learned about God's desires for you?

_____

_____

_____

_____

_____

_____

_____

_____

_____

_____

Day 3

In the Book, <u>Journey from Salvation to Worship</u>, Phase 12 includes several scriptures regarding the Sons of God. What will you do to increase your maturity as a Son of God?

_____

_____

_____

_____

_____

_____

_____

_____

_____

_____

_____

Day 4

How will you "Grow On"?

_____

_____

_____

_____

_____

_____

_____

_____

_____

_____

_____

_____

Day 5

Write a list of all the scriptures, subjects and characters of the Bible you are interested in knowing more about?

_____

_____

_____

_____

_____

_____

_____

_____

_____

_____

_____

Day 6

How will you incorporate daily scripture and study into your schedule?

_____

_____

_____

_____

_____

_____

_____

_____

_____

_____

Day 7

Write the times of the day you commit to read and study your Bible.

_____

_____

_____

_____

_____

_____

_____

_____

_____

_____

Daily Journey Devotion

I will meditate in thy precepts, and have respect unto thy ways. I will delight myself in thy statutes: I will not forget thy word (Psalm 119:15-16).

The scriptures used for your <u>Journey from Salvation to Worship</u> are listed sequentially excluding any repetitions. You may decide to print them and place them in your purse or wallet, create a screensaver for them to read before you begin your day's work, or just open your Bible and read the scriptures page by page. By continuing in devotion, reading selected or spontaneous scriptures help you receive more of God in your Christian experience. Remember to purpose yourself to dedicate at least fifteen (15) minutes each day to read your Bible.

Psalm 91:1-16; 92:1-2
Proverbs 1-31, by day (each chapter)
Romans 8:28-39
Romans 12:1-2
Ephesians 1:15-23; 3:14-21
Ephesians 4:1-6; 6:10-20
2 Corinthians 10:4-5
Philippians 4:4-8
Colossians 3:12-15

References

"Bible Gateway passage: Bible scriptures. King James Version Bible". *Bible Gateway*. N.p., 2017.

"BibleHub Passage: HELPS Study Word". BibleHub. N.p. 2017.

"BibleHub Passage: Mathew Henry Commentary". BibleHub. N.p. 2017.

"BibleHub Passage: New International Version Bible". BibleHub. N.p. 2017.

"BibleHub Passage: New Living Translation". BibleHub. N.p. 2017.

"BibleHub Passage: Strong's Concordance". BibleHub. N.p. 2017.

Moore, DelShanna (2016). Journey from Salvation to Worship. Get Write Publishing, Texas.

In Merriam Webster Online, Retrieved 2017 from http://merriam-webster.com/dictionary.

Nelson, Angie (2017). Biblical Femininity: God's Unique Design for Women. www.calvarychapel.com.

Pittman, Rekesha (2015). Get Write, CHURCH! 7 Steps to Successful Book Publishing. Reignaissance Publications.

Smith, Jay. (2016). Ultimate Bible Summary Collection. Retrieved by biblehub.com.

The Open Bible. New American Standard Bible. Thomas Nelson Publishers, 1977, p. 1227. Retrieved May 2016 by neverthirsty.com.

DelShanna Moore

DelShanna Moore experienced depression, thoughts of suicide, self-destructive behaviors and enticement with perversion and alcohol. She embraces a passion for helping those in need. She humbly serves as an ordained minister and leader. DelShanna facilitates workshops as a pathway to reconciliation, deliverance, and restoration. She exposes God's Word in a way that pierces the stony heart, shatters the walls of alienation and connects you to the freedom granted by the Spirit. DelShanna is a certified Life Coach and achieved dual degrees in Psychology and Public Administration from the University of Nevada Las Vegas.

Reading her book(s), attending her training courses or listening to her speak, leaves you with the phenomenal impression of God's undeniable love and compassion. Receiving divine intervention and 'loosing' captives keep her on her journey while guiding you through your Journey from Salvation to Worship.

**For booking, call (657) 229-HOLY, or
visit www.delshannamoore.com.**

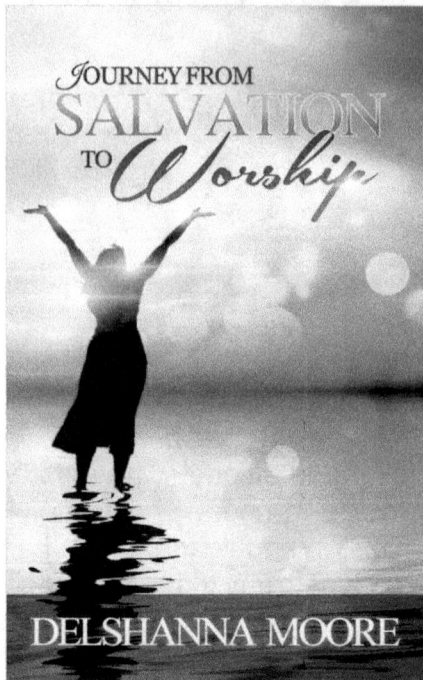

*But without faith
it is impossible to please him:
for he that cometh to God must
believe that he is, and that he is
a rewarder of them that
diligently seek him.
Hebrews 11:6*

www.ingramcontent.com/pod-product-compliance
Lightning Source LLC
LaVergne TN
LVHW021455080426
835509LV00018B/2293